D'Nealian® Handwriting from A to Z

Cursive Capitals Practice

Donald N. Thurber

Good Year Books

An imprint of Pearson Learning
Parsippany, New Jersey

Contents

Good Year Books
are available for most basic curriculum subjects plus many enrichment areas. For more Good Year Books, contact your local bookseller or educational dealer. For a complete catalog with information about other Good Year Books, please write:

Good Year Books
299 Jefferson Road
Parsippany, NJ 07054

Text development by Gerry Murphy-Ferguson.
Book design and art by Nancy Rudd.

D'Nealian® Handwriting is a registered trademark of Donald N. Thurber, licensed exclusively by Scott, Foresman and Company, and is used here with permission.

Copyright © 1987 Scott Foresman and Company. Copyright © 2000 Good Year Books, an imprint of Pearson Learning.

All Rights Reserved.
Printed in the United States of America.

ISBN 0-673-59235-9

2 3 4 5 6 7 8 9–ML–07 06 05 04 03 02 01 00

How to Teach the Letters

Why Teach Capital Letters?

While most adults use manuscript print to fill out forms and make lists, traditionally they use cursive to write personal letters, invitations, and thank-you notes. Just as the conventions of written language apply to manuscript writing, they also apply to cursive. We provided a review of when to use capital letters in an earlier book, *D'Nealian® Handwriting from A to Z: Manuscript Capitals Practice*. We reprint it here for your convenience.

For Your Review

Capital letters are used at the beginning of sentences, for proper nouns such as names, places, organizations, and titles. Children will learn additional uses of capital letters in other Language Arts classes, but for now, we have focused on names, places, organizations, and businesses.

Examples:

At the beginning of sentences: He went to the movies often. Going to the movies is his hobby.

Proper names: Peter Jensen; Barbara Long; Skippy

Places: St. Louis, Missouri; New York, New York; Austin, Texas

Organizations: The American Red Cross; The Parent Teacher Association; Better Business Bureau

Titles: The Secret Garden; Dr. Wendy W. Morgan; Aunt Jane

Beginning writers' needs for knowing when to use capital letters will probably be confined to names and places. Don't overwhelm them at this time in the learning process.

To further help the learner, the capital cursive letters are introduced in common stroke groups—first A, C, E, O; then H, K, N, M, U, V, W, Y; next is T, F, B, P, R; followed by G, S, I; and then a group of letters common only to themselves, Q, Z, D, J, X, L. (If you need to introduce any letters out of this order, just be sure to follow the stroke directions presented on pages 60–61.)

How to Teach Capital Letters

The procedure we suggest for presenting the cursive capital letters is a skill-progressive one. First, ask your child to identify the picture on the first page of each two-page lesson. Spell for your child the word that begins with the capital letter to be introduced, being sure to emphasize the words "Capital A, lower-case p, r, i, l." Have your child repeat after you, pointing to each letter. Next, look at the capital letters in the box to the left. Ask your child if he or she recognizes the first letter in the box. Your child should be able to recognize the manuscript capital letter. Say that the second letter is the cursive form of that letter. Put your hand over the checked response as you discuss if the letters are alike, somewhat alike, or different. After you have discussed and checked your conclusion about the likeness or difference, ask your child to fingertrace the first letter on the writing line below. Have her or him use a pencil to trace the dashed letter. Next, your child should find the starting dots and write single letters without having to trace them. A second line of single-letter practice is provided.

Before your child starts to trace and write the words at the bottom of the first page, you will want to discuss whether or not this capital letter joins to the lowercase letter that follows it. You see that cursive capital A **does** join to the next letter. You should encourage your child to trace the model words first with a pencil or a finger if he or she doesn't write cursive easily. It will help with the flow. After tracing, allow the child to copy the models independently.

The second page of the lesson provides fingertracing, with two words that begin with the capital letter introduced in the lesson. There are Challenge Words at the bottom of the page that the child may write independently. If space is available, your child might want to write the names of friends or pets with that initial letter. They may want to extend this exercise by keeping a list of friends, in alphabetical order, with telephone numbers.

On page 56 is another opportunity to practice writing capital letters in words. You may want to extend the exercise by providing lined paper for personal names and places.

Children are all different. Some need a cheerleader. Some are self-motivating. Some can practice their handwriting for long periods of time, while others are fatigued within a few minutes. It's up to you to know how much practice is good and when practice becomes a drudge. You can make writing easy and fun for your child. Good luck.

April

- [ ] **Alike**
- [ ] **Somewhat alike**
- [x] **Different**

- [x] **Join**
- [ ] **Don't join**

Austin

Alex

Challenge Words

Alaska   *Aaron*   *Allison*

Asia   *Abby*

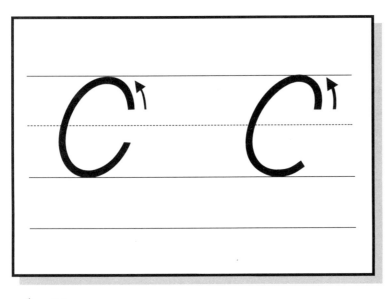

Caitlan

☑ **Alike**
☐ **Somewhat Alike**
☐ **Different**

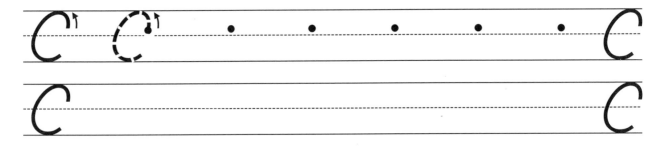

☑ **Join**
☐ **Don't Join**

Caitlan   *Cody*

Camp Cook

Cindy

Carl

Challenge Words

Cuba   *Cathy*   *Curtis*
  Canada   *Cookville*

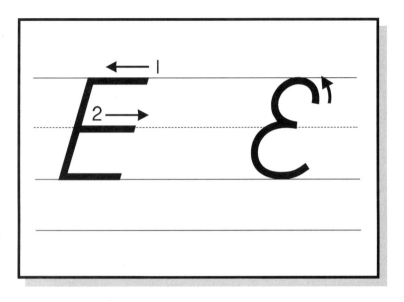

Elm Street

☐ **Alike**
☑ **Somewhat Alike**
☐ **Different**

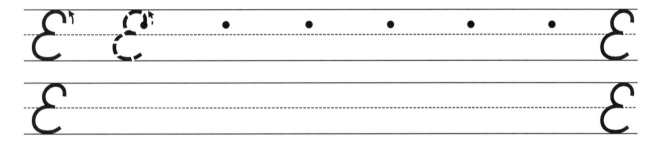

☑ **Join**
☐ **Don't Join**

Ethan   *Erin*

Elm Ave.

Elmo   Edwina

Challenge Words

Europe   Edwin   England

Eleanor   Ely

D'Nealian Handwriting from A to Z: Cursive Capitals Practice   **9**

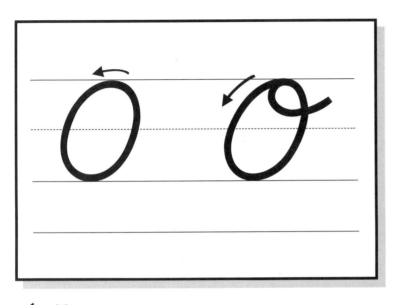

Oliver

- ☑ **Alike**
- ☐ **Somewhat Alike**
- ☐ **Different**

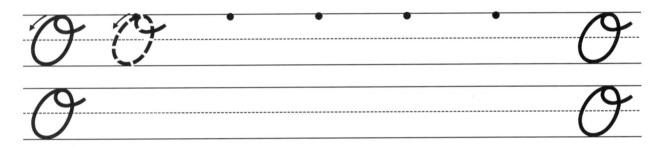

- ☐ **Join**
- ☑ **Don't Join**

Ouida   *Oliver*

Olive Oil

Oona

Otto

Oregon   *Ohio*   *Opal*

Odessa   *Olaf*

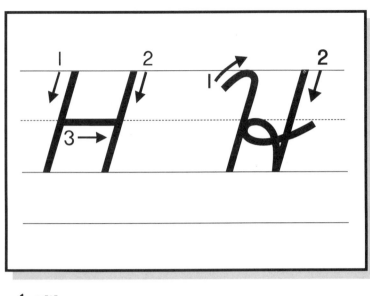

Help!

- ✔ **Alike**
- ☐ **Somewhat Alike**
- ☐ **Different**

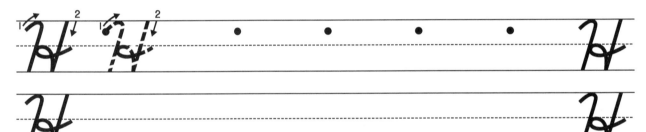

- ☐ **Join**
- ✔ **Don't Join**

Hector   *Helen*

Help!

Heidi   Hutton

Challenge Words

Hawaii   Helena   Harvey

Hank   Hilo

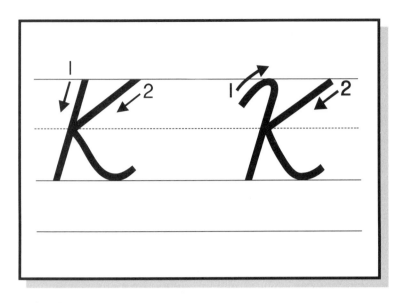

Katie

- ☑ **Alike**
- ☐ **Somewhat Alike**
- ☐ **Different**

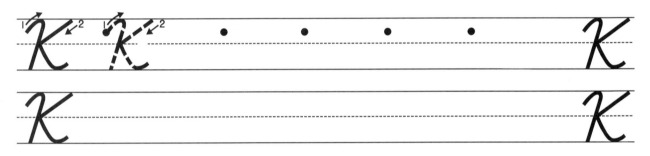

- ☑ **Join**
- ☐ **Don't Join**

Katie   *Kerry*

Kelly Ct.

Kelso   Kirby

Challenge Words

Korea   Kentucky   Kitty

Kenya   Knute

D'Nealian Handwriting from A to Z: Cursive Capitals Practice   **15**

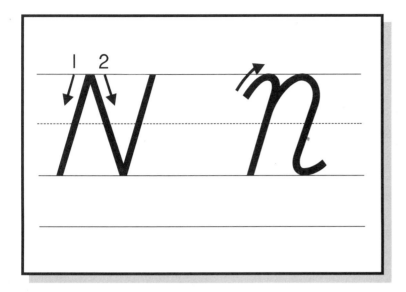

Nob Hill

☐ **Alike**
☑ **Somewhat Alike**
☐ **Different**

n   n   •   •   •   •   n

n   n

☑ **Join**
☐ **Don't Join**

Nathan   Nora

Nob Hill

Neva

Natalie

Challenge Words

Nevada   *Newark*   *Naples*

Nancy   *Newt*

D'Nealian Handwriting from A to Z: Cursive Capitals Practice   **17**

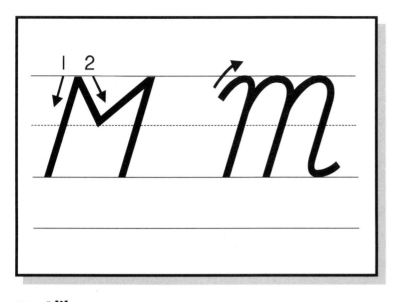

Matt

☐ **Alike**
☑ **Somewhat Alike**
☐ **Different**

☑ **Join**
☐ **Don't Join**

Maggie   *Matt*

Mt. Morris

M m M m

Mora   Mitchell

M   m

M   M

m   m

M   m   M

Challenge Words

Missouri   Maria   Monty
      Marion   Mexico

D'Nealian Handwriting from A to Z: Cursive Capitals Practice   **19**

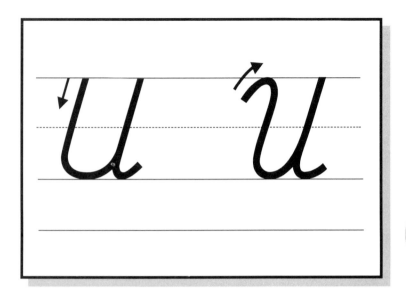

Upton and Ursula

- ✔ **Alike**
- ☐ **Somewhat Alike**
- ☐ **Different**

$\mathcal{U}$ $\mathcal{U}$ • • • • $\mathcal{U}$

$\mathcal{U}$ $\mathcal{U}$

- ✔ **Join**
- ☐ **Don't Join**

Upton *Ursula*

Utah

Ulysses   *Uma*

Challenge Words

Udall   *Utopia*   *Uganda*

Ukraine   *Ulster*

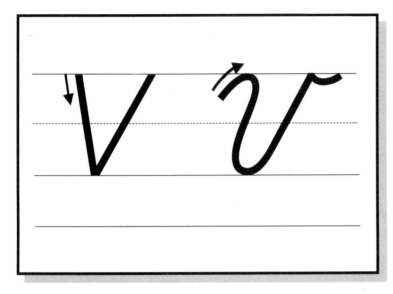

Violet Ave. Florist

☑ **Alike**
☐ **Somewhat Alike**
☐ **Different**

☐ **Join**
☑ **Don't Join**

Vera   *Vic*

Violet Ave.

Veronica   *Vinton*

Challenge Words

Vermont   *Vanna*   *Virgil*

Vernon   *Van*

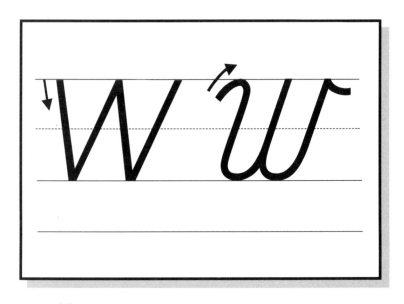

Wilma

☐ **Alike**
☑ **Somewhat Alike**
☐ **Different**

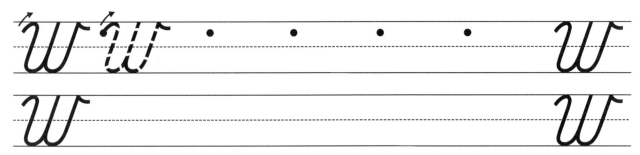

☐ **Join**
☑ **Don't Join**

Waldo   *Wilma*

Western Ave.

Wayne   Wanda

Challenge Words

Waco   Wichita
Winona   Willie

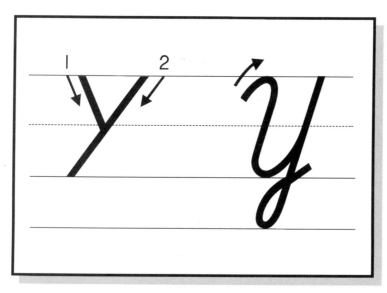

Yves

☐ **Alike**
☑ **Somewhat Alike**
☐ **Different**

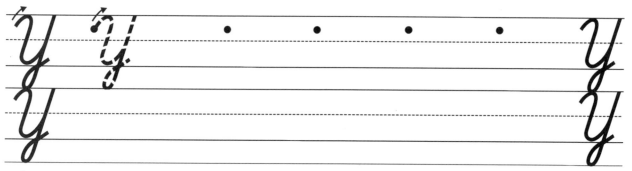

☑ **Join**
☐ **Don't Join**

Yves   *Yves*

Yellowstone

Yolanda   *Yuri*

Challenge Words

Yolene   *Yakima*
Yuma   *Yola*

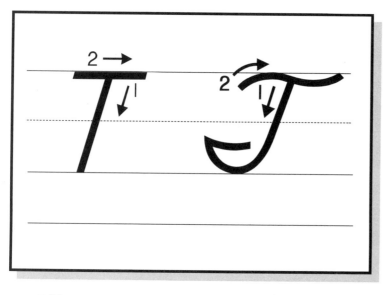

Tacoma

- ☐ **Alike**
- ☑ **Somewhat Alike**
- ☐ **Different**

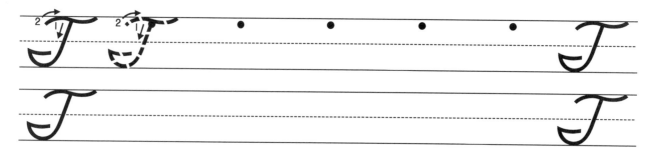

- ☐ **Join**
- ☑ **Don't Join**

Tom   *Tamara*

Tacoma

D'Nealian Handwriting from A to Z: Cursive Capitals Practice

Tweetie   *Tyler*

Challenge Words

Texas   *Tim*   *Tony*

Tanya   *Troy*

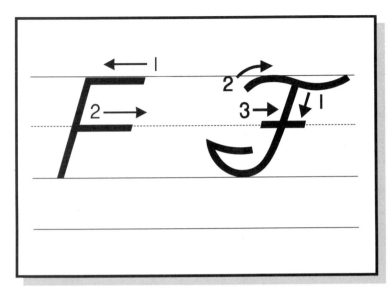

Felicia

☐ **Alike**
☑ **Somewhat Alike**
☐ **Different**

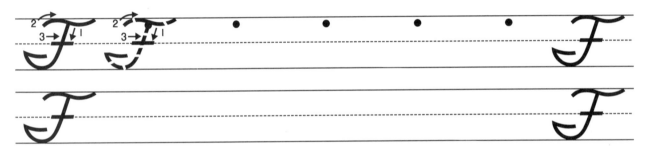

☐ **Join**
☑ **Don't Join**

Felicia   *Fred*

Fourth Ave.

Fern

Frank

Challenge Words

Fresno   Florida   Friday

Fifth Ave.   February

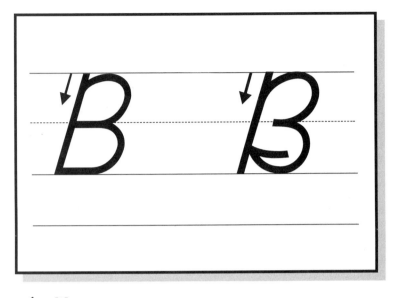

Bonzo

☑ **Alike**
☐ **Somewhat Alike**
☐ **Different**

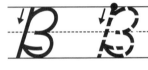

☐ **Join**
☑ **Don't Join**

Brian   *Bev*

Banks Blvd.

Billy

Bonzo

Challenge Words

Boston   *Ben*   *Benji*

Beth   *Baja*

P P

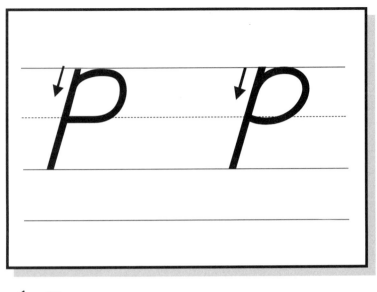

Paolo

☑ **Alike**
☐ **Somewhat Alike**
☐ **Different**

P P   • • • • P

P P

☐ **Join**
☑ **Don't Join**

Pilar   Paolo

Penny Park

Patrick   Peter

Challenge Words

Paris   Perry
Pak   Pocatello

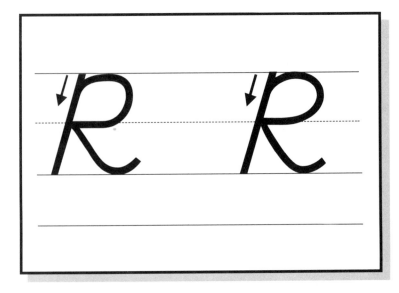

River Road

☑ **Alike**
☐ **Somewhat Alike**
☐ **Different**

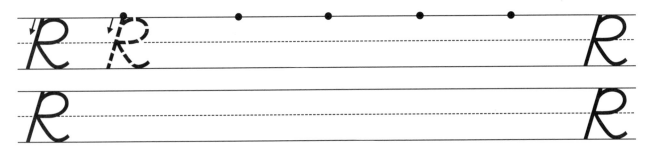

☑ **Join**
☐ **Don't Join**

Roberto   *Rena*

River Road

Robin　　　　Ruth

Challenge Words

Russia　　　Rosita　　　Raleigh

Mt. Rushmore　　　Ronan

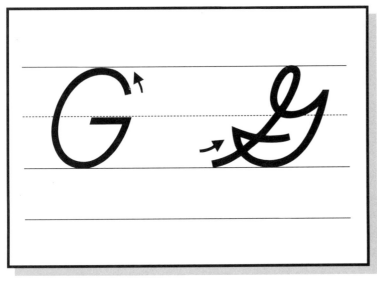

Gigi

☐ **Alike**
☐ **Somewhat Alike**
✔ **Different**

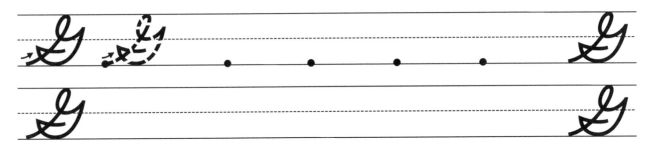

☐ **Join**
✔ **Don't Join**

Gigi   *Geoff*

Gull Ave.

Gibson

Gill

Challenge Words

Georgia

German

Gary

Gerry

Garth

D'Nealian Handwriting from A to Z: Cursive Capitals Practice **39**

Samuel

- ☐ **Alike**
- ☐ **Somewhat Alike**
- ☑ **Different**

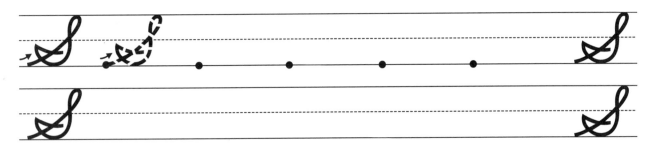

- ☐ **Join**
- ☑ **Don't Join**

Sara   Samuel

Sandy St.

Sue

Sid

Challenge Words

Spain   Seattle   Sumi

Sol   Sally

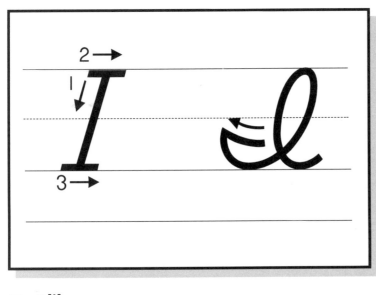

Iggy

☐ **Alike**
☐ **Somewhat Alike**
☑ **Different**

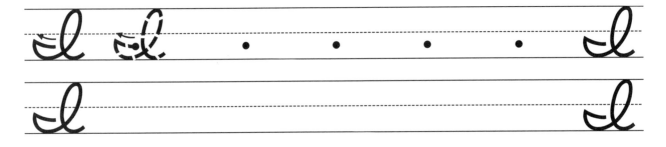

☑ **Join**
☐ **Don't Join**

Inez

Iggy

Inca Ct.

D'Nealian Handwriting from A to Z: Cursive Capitals Practice

Iris

Ira

Challenge Words

Ireland   *Irish*   *Ito*

Israel   *Idaho*

D'Nealian Handwriting from A to Z: Cursive Capitals Practice   **43**

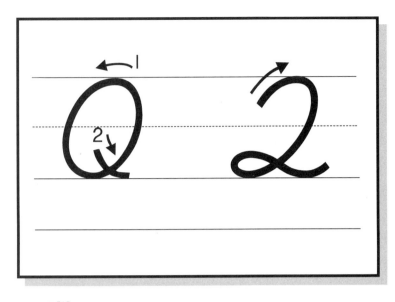

Quin

☐ **Alike**
☐ **Somewhat Alike**
☑ **Different**

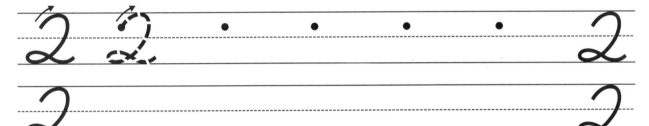

☑ **Join**
☐ **Don't Join**

Quentin   *Quin*

Quilt Ave.

Quincy   *Quint*

Challenge Words

Qatar   *Quebec*

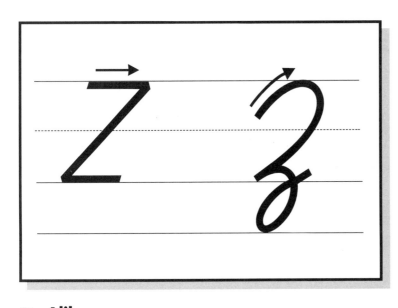

Zeb

☐ **Alike**
☐ **Somewhat Alike**
☑ **Different**

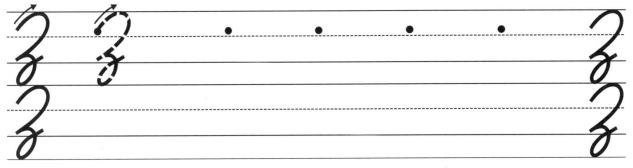

☑ **Join**
☐ **Don't Join**

Zoe   *Zeb*

Zone St.

Zola

Zelda

Zimbabwe

Zanzibar

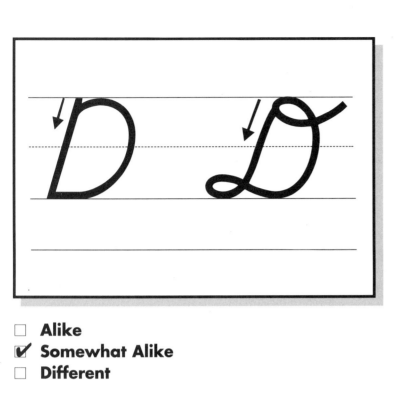

Daniel

☐ **Alike**
☑ **Somewhat Alike**
☐ **Different**

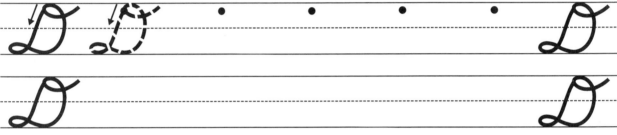

☐ **Join**
☑ **Don't Join**

Daniel   *Donna*

Dave Dr.

Dawn

Derrick

Denver   *Dover*   *Delores*

Dante   *Dean*

D'Nealian Handwriting from A to Z: Cursive Capitals Practice   **49**

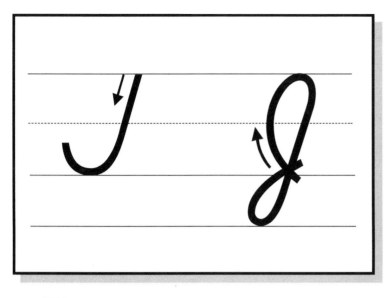

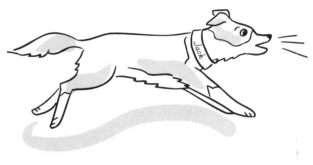

Jack

- ☐ **Alike**
- ☐ **Somewhat Alike**
- ☑ **Different**

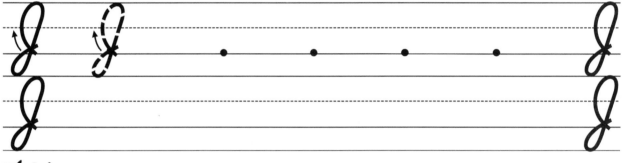

- ☑ **Join**
- ☐ **Don't Join**

Jolene   *Jack*

Juniper Ln.

Joyce

Joey

Challenge Words

Japan

Jamaica

Jane

Joan

Julie

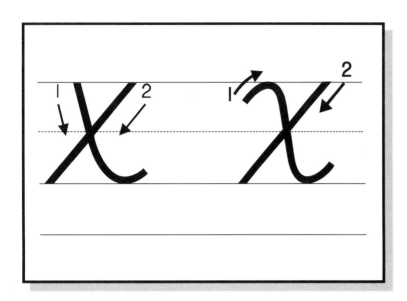

Xenia Square

☑ **Alike**
☐ **Somewhat Alike**
☐ **Different**

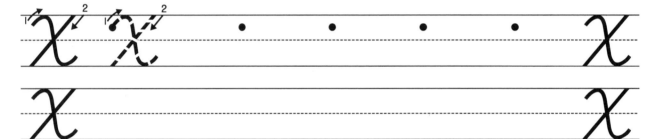

☐ **Join**
☑ **Don't Join**

Xavier

Xenia Square

X-ray   *Xmas*

Xerox Park

Louis

☐ **Alike**
☑ **Somewhat Alike**
☐ **Different**

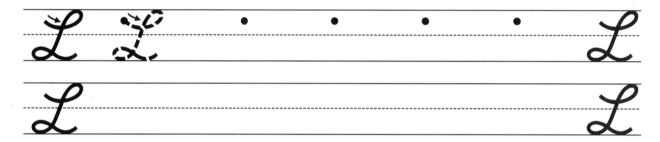

☑ **Join**
☐ **Don't Join**

Lin   *Louis*

La Belle Ln.

Libby *Lenard*

Challenge Words

London *Lamar* *Lincoln*

Lakeview *Lenny*

D'Nealian Handwriting from A to Z: Cursive Capitals Practice **55**

Two Ways to Write

manuscript   cursive

Alaska   *Alaska*

Boston   *Boston*

Chicago   *Chicago*

Detroit   *Detroit*

Edward   *Edward*

manuscript	cursive
Florida	Florida
Grant	Grant
Herbie	Herbie
Iris	Iris
January	January

manuscript	cursive
Kato	Kato
Laramie	Laramie
Monday	Monday
November	November
Omaha	Omaha

Two Ways to Write

manuscript   cursive

Park Place   Park Place

Quincy   Quincy

Roberto   Roberto

Seattle   Seattle

Trenton   Trenton

Directions for Forming the Letters

A   Top start; around down, close up, down, and up.

B   Top start; down, up, around halfway, around again, touch, sidestroke, and stop.

C   Start below the top; curve up, around, down, and up.

D   Top start; down, loop right, curve up, around, close, loop right, through, and stop.

E   Start below the top; curve up, around to the middle, around again to the bottom line, and up.

F   Start below the top; down, around and sidestroke. Wavy cross and a cross.

G   Bottom start; uphill high, loop through the middle, up, curve down, around, through the uphill, sidestroke, and stop.

H   Start below the top; make a cane. Top start, to the right; down, up, left, touch, loop right, through, and stop.

I   Start below the middle; sidestroke, curve down, around, uphill high, loop down, and up.

J   Bottom start; curve up, around, touch on the way down under water, loop up left, and through.

K   Start below the top; make a cane. Top start, to the right; slant down left, touch, slant down right, and up.

L   Start below the top; uphill, loop down, loop right, and up.

M   Start below the top; make a cane, up over the hill, up over the hill again, and up.

N   Start below the top; make a cane, up over the hill, and up.

O   Top start; around down, close up, right, through, and stop.

P   Top start; down, up, around halfway, and close.

Q   Start below the top; curve up, around, down, loop right, and up.

R   Top start; down, up, around halfway, close, slant down right, and up.

S   Bottom start; uphill high, loop through the middle, curve down, around through the uphill, sidestroke, and stop.

T   Start below the top; down, around, up and sidestroke. Wavy cross.

U   Start below the top; make a cane, around up, down, and up.

V   Start below the top; make a cane, around, slant up right, sidestroke, and stop.

W   Start below the top; make a cane, around, up, down, around, up again, sidestroke, and stop.

X   Start below the top; curve up, slant right, and up. Cross down left.

Y   Start below the top; make a cane, around, up down under water, loop up left, and through.

Z   Start below the top; curve up, around, down, around again, and down under water, loop up left, and through.

$\mathcal{A}$ $\mathcal{A}$ $\mathcal{A}$ $\mathcal{A}$ $\mathcal{A}$ $\mathcal{A}$ $\mathcal{A}$

$\mathcal{B}$ $\mathcal{B}$ $\mathcal{B}$ $\mathcal{B}$ $\mathcal{B}$ $\mathcal{B}$ $\mathcal{B}$

$\mathcal{C}$ $\mathcal{C}$ $\mathcal{C}$ $\mathcal{C}$ $\mathcal{C}$ $\mathcal{C}$ $\mathcal{C}$

$\mathcal{D}$ $\mathcal{D}$ $\mathcal{D}$ $\mathcal{D}$ $\mathcal{D}$ $\mathcal{D}$ $\mathcal{D}$

$\mathcal{E}$ $\mathcal{E}$ $\mathcal{E}$ $\mathcal{E}$ $\mathcal{E}$ $\mathcal{E}$ $\mathcal{E}$

$\mathcal{F}$ $\mathcal{F}$ $\mathcal{F}$ $\mathcal{F}$ $\mathcal{F}$ $\mathcal{F}$ $\mathcal{F}$

$\mathcal{G}$ $\mathcal{G}$ $\mathcal{G}$ $\mathcal{G}$ $\mathcal{G}$ $\mathcal{G}$ $\mathcal{G}$

$\mathcal{H}$ $\mathcal{H}$ $\mathcal{H}$ $\mathcal{H}$ $\mathcal{H}$ $\mathcal{H}$ $\mathcal{H}$

$\mathcal{I}$ $\mathcal{I}$ $\mathcal{I}$ $\mathcal{I}$ $\mathcal{I}$ $\mathcal{I}$ $\mathcal{I}$

$\mathcal{J}$ $\mathcal{J}$ $\mathcal{J}$ $\mathcal{J}$ $\mathcal{J}$ $\mathcal{J}$ $\mathcal{J}$

$\mathcal{K}$ $\mathcal{K}$ $\mathcal{K}$ $\mathcal{K}$ $\mathcal{K}$ $\mathcal{K}$ $\mathcal{K}$

$\mathcal{L}$ $\mathcal{L}$ $\mathcal{L}$ $\mathcal{L}$ $\mathcal{L}$ $\mathcal{L}$ $\mathcal{L}$

$\mathcal{M}$ $\mathcal{M}$ $\mathcal{M}$ $\mathcal{M}$ $\mathcal{M}$ $\mathcal{M}$ $\mathcal{M}$

n n n n n n n

o o o o o o o

P P P P P P P

2 2 2 2 2 2 2

R R R R R R R

J J J J J J J

T T T T T T T

U U U U U U U

V V V V V V V

W W W W W W W

X X X X X X X

Y Y Y Y Y Y Y

Z Z Z Z Z Z Z